LOOK AND SEE

The Story of Jesus

Johannas.

Leena Lane and Moira Maclean

Jesus is born

Look! Here is Jesus.
Mary and Joseph look after him,
but Jesus is God's son.
An angel told Mary she would have a baby.
She should call the baby Jesus.
Jesus was born in the town of Bethlehem.
One day, some wise men followed a bright star
to find the special child born to be King.
First of all, they went to King Herod's palace,
but the baby was not there.
God's son was not born in a palace!
The wise men followed the star.
They found Jesus in Bethlehem
with Joseph, and Mary his mother.
The wise men brought gifts for Jesus:
gold, sweet smelling frankincense and myrrh.
They knelt down and worshipped him,
but they didn't tell King Herod where he was!
They went back home by a different road.

How many gifts have the wise men brought?

John the Baptist

Look! Here is John the Baptist.
John ate locusts and honey.
He wore rough clothes.
John told everyone about Jesus.
'Say sorry to God,' he said.
'Jesus is coming. Get ready for him.'
John baptised people in the river.
He prayed for them.
One day Jesus came to see John.
Jesus had grown up into a man now.
'Baptise me, John,' said Jesus.
John was very surprised.
But he baptised Jesus in the river.
Then a voice from heaven spoke:
'This is my son; I am pleased with him.'
It was God speaking!
The Holy Spirit came like a dove.
John knew that Jesus is God's own son.

Can you see the dove?

Jesus' disciples

Look! Here are Peter and Andrew.
Peter and Andrew were fishermen.
They were casting their net into the lake
when Jesus walked by.
He wanted them to be his friends.
'Come and follow me!' said Jesus.
'I will make you fishers of people.'
Peter and Andrew left their nets.
They followed Jesus when he called them.
Jesus saw James and John.
They were fishermen too.
'Come with me!' says Jesus.
'Be my disciples.'
James and John left their nets.
They followed Jesus, too.
Peter, Andrew, James and John
were Jesus' first disciples.

Can you see the fish in the basket?

The wedding in Cana

Look! Here is Jesus.
He has gone to a wedding feast.
Mary went with Jesus.
While they were there, the wine ran out.
There was no more wine for the feast.
Jesus knew what to do.
He talked to the servants:
'Fill up six large jars with water.'
The servants did as he asked.
'Now take some out.
Give it to the master of the feast.'
When the servant poured the water,
it had turned into wine!
The master was very pleased.
'You have saved the best t'il last!' he said.
Jesus had worked a miracle.
He changed water into wine.

Can you count the water jars?

The storm

Look! Here is Jesus.
He sailed across the lake in a boat.
His disciples were with him.
Jesus was tired and fell asleep.
Suddenly the wind started to blow.
The thunder rolled and lightning flashed.
It was a storm!
But Jesus was still asleep.
His disciples were very scared.
'Wake up, Jesus!' they shouted.
'Save us! We're going to drown!'
Jesus heard them and woke up.
'Why are you so frightened?' he asked.
Jesus stood up and told the storm to stop.
The wind dropped and it was calm again.
The disciples were amazed.
Jesus had calmed the storm!

Can you see the lightning flashing?

Jesus feeds a huge crowd

Look! Here is a hungry crowd.
The people were listening to Jesus.
When it was time to eat,
there was nowhere to buy food.
'What can the people eat?'
Jesus asked his disciples.
Andrew spoke up: 'There is a boy here.
He has two small loaves and five fishes.
But how can that feed so many?'
Jesus took the food and thanked God for it.
He broke it into pieces and handed it round.
Everyone ate; everyone shared.
Everyone had enough and no one was hungry!
There was even food left over.
The disciples gathered up what was left
and filled twelve baskets!
Jesus had fed more than 5000 people!
It was a miracle.

Can you count the birds in the sky?

Jesus comes to Jerusalem

Look! Here is Jesus.
He is riding on a donkey.
Jesus was coming to Jerusalem.
People were following him.
People were waiting for him.
They stood at the roadside.
Jesus had made people well.
Jesus had told wonderful stories.
Jesus had taught them about God.
He had turned water into wine,
he had calmed a storm
and he had fed hungry people.
People waved huge palm branches.
They threw down their cloaks.
Jesus, their King, was riding by.
'Hosanna!' they shouted. 'Thank you, God!'
They waved and cheered for Jesus.

Can you count the palm branches?

Jesus eats with his friends

Look! Here are twelve disciples.
They are having a meal with Jesus.
It was the Passover meal
of lamb and herbs, bread and wine.
But Jesus was sad.
Soon he would be taken from his disciples.
Jesus took the bread
and thanked God for it.
He broke it into pieces
and shared it with his friends.
'Remember me whenever
you eat bread like this,' he said.
Then Jesus took the wine.
'Remember me whenever
you drink wine like this,' he said.
Judas Iscariot was one of the disciples.
Judas was no longer Jesus' friend.
He left to tell the guards how to capture Jesus.

Can you see the bread and wine?

Jesus dies on a cross

Look! Here is Jesus.
Jesus is on a cross on a hillside.
Jesus did nothing wrong.
But he was taken away by soldiers.
Jesus was nailed to a cross.
Two robbers were next to him.
Jesus' friends were watching.
Jesus' mother was watching.
They were very, very sad.
Why must Jesus be hurt?
The sky turned black.
Jesus cried out to God in a loud voice.
Then Jesus died.
Jesus' body was taken down from the cross.
It was carried away and buried in a rock tomb.
A big stone was rolled across the doorway.
It was a terrible day for all his friends.

Can you see Mary weeping?

Jesus is alive!

Look! Here is Mary.
She is going to Jesus' tomb.
Mary was very sad.
She loved Jesus.
Now he was dead.
She came with herbs and spices.
Here is the tomb.
But what's this?
The big stone has been rolled away.
The tomb is empty!
Where is Jesus?
Two angels appear.
'Jesus is alive!' they say.
'Go and tell everyone!'
Mary runs as fast as she can.
'Jesus is alive!' she shouts.
It is a wonderful day!

Can you see the stone which is rolled away?

Jesus meets his friends again

Look! Here are the fishermen.
They are Jesus' disciples.
They have been fishing all night but caught nothing.
Look! Here is Jesus!
He is watching from the shore.
'Throw your nets out on the other side!' he shouts.
The disciples do as he says.
Their nets nearly break with all the fish!
'Can it be Jesus?' John asks.
It was! The disciples were amazed.
They pulled in their catch and went to see Jesus.
He was cooking bread and fish for them.
They talked and ate together.
Jesus died but he was really alive again.
Soon he would return to be with God in heaven.
But Jesus promised he would be with them
and would never leave them again.

Can you see the fire on the beach?

Published in the UK by
The Bible Reading Fellowship
First Floor, Elsfield Hall, 15-17 Elsfield Way, Oxford OX2 8FG
ISBN 1 84101 412 5

First edition 2005

Copyright © 2005 AD Publishing Services Ltd
1 Churchgates, The Wilderness, Berkhamsted, Herts HP4 2UB
Text copyright © 2005 AD Publishing Services Ltd, Leena Lane
Illustrations copyright © 2005 Moira Maclean

Editorial Director Annette Reynolds
Art Director Gerald Rogers
Pre-production Krystyna Hewitt
Production John Laister

British Library Cataloguing in Publication Data.
A catalogue record for this book is available from the
British Library.

Printed and bound in Singapore